© 2025 by Yon Walls

All rights reserved. No part of this book may be reproduced in any form or by any means without the prior written consent of the publisher, except for brief quotes used in reviews.

ISBN-13: 978-0-9903095-4-3 (paperback)
ISBN-13: 978-0-9903095-5-0 (hardcover)

Copyediting, production, and design by Joanne Shwed, Backspace Ink (www.backspaceink.com)

Photo credit by Wayne A. Moody

Flowers of Diagnosis

New and Selected Poems

YON WALLS

to the muses ...

My world did not shrink because I was a Black female writer. It just got bigger.
—Toni Morrison

CONTENTS

PART I 11

1999–2021 13

    Migration 15

    Black, Gray and Mauve 18

    Religion 19

    The Last Language 22

    Dreamscape 24

    How to Celebrate the Moon 26

    Self-Study 28

    Loving and Limits 29

    Making an Image 30

    Argentine Bloom 31

    Health Psychology 32

    Seeing a Flower That Way 34

    Flowers of Diagnosis 35

PART II 37

Japan, 2002–2007 39

    Rehearsal: Pears and Cellos 41

    Dazai's Mermaid 42

    Floating 43

    Hiroshima Girls 44

    To Imbe 45

    Summer Death 46

    Kazo *Itoh* 47

    Wild Boor 48

    Bon Odori 49

    Radiation 50

    Samurai's Tea 51

City Sight 52

Island of Swallows 53

Ginza in June 54

Katsunama: Wine Country 55

Sleep 56

Anticipation 57

New Plums 58

Hiroshima Bridge 60

Sadako's Riddle 61

Masahiro's Beach 62

Dinner Guest 63

Nearly Christmas 64

Tea Lesson at Dusk 65

Autumn Comes 66

Winter: Learning to Be Tough 67

Rebel 68

The Kimono Maker 69

Dialogues 72

Geisha's Discovery 78

Sunlight from the North View 79

At Recital 80

Kyoto 81

Intersection 82

PART III 83

San Francisco, 1993–2000 85

Mills College: Contemplating Pottery 87

Gathering 88

Mei Lei (1967) 89

Excavating Water; Ars Poetica 90

Reading Prose 91

Twin Artifact 92

Like Lantern 93

A Wedding Song 94

Near Seven 95

1966 96

Nella's Eyes 97

On the Island 98

Autumn Landscape 101

Following Spring Path 103

Kentucky Sunflower 105

Pretty Women 106

To Be Afraid 107

Divorce Elegy 108

Chance 109

Poet to Student 110

Rites of Passage 111

GLOSSARY 113

AUTHOR'S BIO 115

PART I

1999–2021

MIGRATION

I.

Yesterday I found my body then
Lost it,
Had scent of you,
Your warm flesh

When your daughter
I hadn't remembered it,
But now,
Sensory
And solid
As meeting a
Bare tree
In December.

Being in that moment
I knew you
Again
You called out
To come
Back, smiling

And then,
You vanished,
As a noble grain
Of salt.

II.

It was a strong trembling,
A grieving lapis heart
That pulsed in the night,
Deeper than
A feathery whisper.
It gently
Ran away with me
Entered,
And I surrendered
Lost,
And then discovered
On a soft-sanded beach
Covered
By fairy light.

III.

Hold my hand.
The skin fever is persistent; travailing
New territory
In strong, impatient fits.

Heat of different colors
Calling name
As if new,
In moments of twisting river,
And fire language.

Bodies know satiation—
Lush chambers
Of opening,
Wide-awakeness rehearsing the look

Of a ripe season,
And drawings imprinted
For love.

BLACK, GRAY AND MAUVE

The flattening October air tapestry
Across the dawn rising;
Enlivening here, there—
A vined wall, half asleep.

Unchanging grey—
A radiant dullness then; shell, white, violet
Seeping through,
Earth-*ing* us
For the coming season.

RELIGION

I.

Till the day
And the soul-silvered silence
When all doctrine
Rings untrue: What is searched for?
A god
More powerful than the body's
Ability to hold itself
As the integrated system of eons
With bone, blood
And electricity
    That mends together—
        Cradles us true and binding
Despite any wars.

II.

And then a day
Of tricky reckoning—
A hot cruelty that teaches
How formidable god really is—
How fragile
The agreement
To love despite the weighted hours
That teach
Material raw philosophy,
Agony
And high-spiritedness.

III.

Called the something beyond
That our muscles crave
And deepen
Into our lives
With the stretching inward
Until you know
That hearts
Do break and shatter
     And find true religion
        Found by a burning foreign name
Solid and forever
Ephemeral.

IV.

Pre-personality we become
Learning the organic power
Of rock, water, sky
And feces
Recycled as something
We just recognize
And smell for ourselves
That no doctrine
Can explain
From a spasm
Of arabesque
Tears—
That clarity
Of our constellation and orbits
That teaches us
Real space and fluid time.

Again until we too
Will climb
The trellis of marbled grief
And become,
The thing we lost.

THE LAST LANGUAGE

I.

Abruptly—
the plum branches
know our childhood
before death;
stem, leaf
down to the stubborn
root,
our circle
        of mother daughter
hands
and architecture of sort
celebrating blood—
the sky as changeling
into new fire
of lost speech
and beginning tongue.

II.

First tears
In fluid body
trying
to reason
from dying molecules
face—
frozen, throat trembling
beautiful us.

III.

Our basket open
with good design,
composition of syllables
for a playful afterlife.

IV.

Raw
across the tender
generations.
Now, her halo
an unfathomable
grace.

DREAMSCAPE

(1)

Ask me once
and I won't tell
ask me twice
and a stone,
but the river is flowing
both ways

(2)

Whir me around
to all
the places
I don't know,
give me color
I can sing—
you can sing
these colors
now,
I've never
seen

(3)

This heart
of machine
in time—
a little time
that demands this moment—
form, feeling
and reach,

I am
now the heart,
the deeper part
that has
no form

(4)

Fire of life
opens
to me,
builds from the muscle
of happening
in a capsule—
the garden
gate

(5)

Center me--
yoke of patchwork,
the yellow pasty love
that I call myself.
A hand of compassion--
the eye
of this hot wisdom
that smells of knowing
like fresh fruit

HOW TO CELEBRATE THE MOON

When we
Don't watch its waxy comeliness anymore
From the cool bathroom window
Or out among the garden vines
To chase it further back
Into the deeper jet sky
To *see* it better,
The transition object that never
Leaves the transitional body
Changing as fast as a bird's
Turn of song
As ice melting.

It is there
Because we need to find it, every time
No matter how well we know it
As new constellations erupt in our hearts,
Knitting and reknitting our souls
Patient for the darkness to pass and the incubating life
To make us fearless;
For new dreams, ears, new
Skin to feel with.

It is our
Sky candy, shiny and lustrous
From season to season, telling us
Mythical and faraway stories, showing us how to be
Just still
To honor the refrain and
To pray.

It is our antique sky-maker
And our long-ago
Cells and tissue that remember
All that happened
Where they were
And what they cast away
For love.

SELF-STUDY

Almost the year I didn't plan for
And think about when the body was on the edge
Of opening
And revelations and unexperienced narratives
Then,

Now, something is less anticipated
With sinew of movement and reaching
For something closer
Than a long next era looking
Forward.

Facial recognition just found?
Or that fresh then deepening face hiding
From itself.

This precipice year of a less
Certain body and celebration despite
The illusion of something
That settles—something
To bank on
Now, the body
Unholding.

LOVING AND LIMITS

However you want
To put it, *yes* will defy *no* every time
Because *supposed to* is better;
In history
The heroes and heroines who
Continue the tribe—
The race
Fighting for boundary
Soil, place.

And *no* is suffering for
Something deserved or at least
A measure
And I say *yes*, and the days before
When *no*
Taught me to stand up
To it.

Because the soul seeks pleasure
When we
Least expect it
When *yes* by its nature
Is space and a view
To muse about.

MAKING AN IMAGE

He captures images
Like a youthful mystic who will soon
Die, almost desperate
For each summer day at sunrise
The garden—
A sparkling affair
In hidden sight.

Medicine for a survivor
The body's episode that came
And took its
Toll
As if the trees, scrubs, the thick tangle
Of tendril and bloom
Predestined it all—
A sharp cut through brave flesh.
Breathing those moments
To discover something missed, forgotten
Or like an exotic place
Never traveled to before
On a blue, slender boat.

He takes it all in
With the lens like a master
At feast
Knowing the balance of things;
A tightrope walker, a dancer in the dark
And the day opens
Cool, hot, cool
With gratitude.

ARGENTINE BLOOM

This curious season
The cactus
Have flowered.

The whiter than
White blooms
For a brief time
Stretch, opening
And conversation
Like Romans at bath.

Almost too much
A show—
A theatrical perfection
Basking in the glow.

Nightfall soon
The feathery spiky blooms
As prophetic ancient calendars
Recede from sun
In temporary ancient
Darkness.

Narrative of something
Intimate
And closing
Bloom retreating less milky
A sharp farewell;
The stem naked
And Depleted.

HEALTH PSYCHOLOGY

At this point
In early July
The learning has *unlearned* me—
A rebellion against diagnosis as something
Humans can use.

Up from the ground like a bulb
Deep roots
This thing can spring,
The hard life's lesson, resistance to something
The skillful swimmer
Who is always diving for something
At no bottom.

This disease of life
Can't be pointed to as a threatening malady
When something else
Is there too—
The *real* cause
The one that looks us in the face
And laughs.

An analysis of disease—
A brilliant lover who gets the rhythm of pleasure
Fast, and the pain
That can only equal it
To teach contrast—
The price for living deeply, angrily—
Sometimes a deaf mute
When the wounds are fresh
And unlooked after.

How can it be healed?
A medicine, a word
Just speaking its name honestly
As a tree that survives
To make roots
Or the insect
That eats it.

SEEING A FLOWER THAT WAY
For the three-year-old

Not for putting in my mouth
Not for throwing
Or chasing.

It's bright yellow and alive;
Mommy gives it to me.

It's for seeing, for touching this
Spiky, surprising thing—
This flower I can
Hold and smell in my hand.

Like this,
Just now I can see
Everything.

FLOWERS OF DIAGNOSIS

The rose bush
Relishes the sun, and it
Buds
Heavy and lush
From the nurtured soil,
Like a couple in spring and the flowing days
Because of love
And then, spreading
Into the body organ—
The unexpected sexual diagnosis.
It doesn't take all,
Just a slow unrooting despite,
Resistance and grief entwined
That leaves the body
To wonder
And hateful buds
That bloomed one season for them
Because of love.

PART II

Japan, 2002–2007

How invisibly it changes color,
In this world,
The flower
Of the human heart.
—Ono No Komachi (8th century)

REHEARSAL: PEARS AND CELLOS

Ancient spring children
        Unfold
Into flat wedges
Of origami—
Two anatomies
Of old cello—
And the ripened pear
That Michelangelo didn't paint
And her un-simple meal
Playful
        then a skillful tune
On the seihakuji.

Yet a wilder pitch than sweet
        A thinking of cedar
        And luck unrhymed
        And strings of bitter
And something binding—
A sonnet.

DAZAI'S MERMAID
For Osamu Dazai (1909-1948)

The classic tale
Tells that the Mermaid's
      "body was transparent
crystal with a slight bluish tinge
its breasts were two red berries
of the nandina bamboo,"
an ingénue enslaved
by an effete sea god—
the precocious task
of delivering an omen.

She not a guardian
or a seaman's enchantment.
A prized shoulder wound and death
by a fishmonger's arrow
proves her insane.
At death
he becomes half-man,
a wounded fish,
part arrow.

FLOATING

Seto bowl is purified
Under bright-lit moon, by sure hands, a will—
A spirit moved.

And another quarter turn
A bow, wrist—
A summer passed too quickly.

HIROSHIMA GIRLS

The twins carelessly pose on Tuesday—
one fashioned the air of a long-necked crane
the younger one a festival
of silk balls. They become the multireflected
window as the stranger joins in their gaiety, steadying to press
the shutter as they shine through
an interstice of ripe adolescence.
Impatiently they smile—
swift as the passing of sakura
a demand of perfect
folds and a plethora of knots—
ties as ancestors. Arching toward the clear
glass, they pique the lens
and open.

TO IMBE
for john and betsy

the drive continues into the almost-autumn mountains
that look like
old Chinese oil paintings,
ripened persimmon swing
so low on its branches
they obscure
the heroics of several stone cottages.

She says: *The kaki are everywhere*
as heavier branches dot the journey—
and then she mentions crows and fermenting dumps
extinguishing the image
of the fire branches.

But ravens
Are the most resourceful
she seems to think, and talks of the Inuit
and their belief that they are transformers
as there appears a coppice of black bamboo.

There is talk of the neighborhood sakana-ya
and the roasting of living crustaceans—
the memory of recognition
the deaf struggle of tentacles,
and lusty communion.

SUMMER DEATH

      That steel-blue door
And that almost falling red sunset—
frigid, a thing rotting,
clinging to the bile of Earth,
a womb hard, and still and dead.

The swallow's nest resists the hand
to destroy it
After the sharpest blow—
dust like flame,
its quixotic paper wings
a chimera
hanging in air
afferent to the force
of its destruction—

a face, and flies
into the fleeing night.

KAZO *ITOH*

Edo quarters stretch back in time—
A charred sky under slow simmer
Desires held and loosed
By the local man's
Words: *over the river.*

His kibishi introduction
As the island man
Itoh; a prominent linage—speaking a different dialect,
As the curious
Lovers await the sour soup with Bok Choy
Tangling,
Two sakana in fresh water.
      Here we say: oki ni
As a lover strokes
A miniature kabin from myriad photos,
They agree like silk
In the night: *this one*
The expression on her face,
the red obi.

WILD BOOR

The squeal—
the sound of agonies of fighting boors
locking and tearing
from soil—evokes a strange pleasure in the dense night.
The dominant boor awaits the next flight;
the leap into flesh, the taste—
trembling.

Throated sirens continue into the humid hours
Suddenly, an apparition—
the recognition of a human
In search of wild meat
in the daikon garden
near the gold shrine.

BON ODORI

You look lovely in kimono, I say to her—
the horizontal lines and naïve spray of flowers
seem becoming.
The music slowly draws the elders
into the sand-swept circle—
children of mochi,
gaggles of balls and dolls
fashioned as ceremonial relics. All join
to be possessed as first children as the taiko unwind
the center of earth like ribbon.
        The dance requires the arms
to conform to sky
to form as half crosses, arcs and then
rectangles in the soft night.

Fluidly, Chinami with the ease of a native
calculates three steps and turns her hips like flashing
the edge of a sharp sword—
a wail of the singer's voice then enters her body
as a welcomed ghost.
        The fragile-boned elder looks into
the eyes of the foreigner: kore here, she utters,
pointing to the pattern of her feet, for the stranger
follow until the ghost enters
and possession.
Then by quashes of light her movements
show the struggle of something
to be lifted, a swift elegance
and the erotic
of the whole.

RADIATION

In the night cracking the silence
And restless body:
What do you smell like
After treatment? Like metal?
This hour is not a time for lovers
At the foot of Mt. Fuji
Or a valley back home. And the vision of lips
And lock of hair and musky sweetness comes:
This blood and skin and organ
That defy gamma rays—
And touch the deepest
Garden of blooming foliage—
Of a worker's hand,
Of hard earth—
Dying matter and stone,
As light as paper
On fire the first
Star between them.

SAMURAI'S TEA

Shoji screens block full view
of the damp garden—
the scattered lotus- and emerald-swept moss.
      The small circle of Tokiko's friends, after the washing
at the chozubashi, await the New Year's gift with matcha:
softly boiled, two beans; the large, black one
adzuki and the scenic chawan.

The wailing silence
Calls up the intersection of
Two worlds—the black ink of myth
No beginning, no end.

The tea is served from one bowl, consumed thick and slow
Bitter and sweet.

CITY SIGHT

The head of the shrine sparkles from the vantage point
of coming up the avenue to the crest
of the northernmost point.
        The bridge is painted a Chinese red
and white swan, heron
and small tortoises swim on the pattern of roof.

A shop owner
Is busy with his goods—
wines, the jellies, ice cream
and the warlord's memorabilia.
        Across the portal past the newly crafted
Noh stage
is the chamber of mirrors
that reflects a view
of all visiting souls who look at them
        And near the oak.
with lichen near the small museum
is the mechanical fortune-teller
who tells a fortune: *a good heart*
For all things social—
The temperament of an old, wise man—
Wit and melancholy
like stone.

ISLAND OF SWALLOWS

On the island
The shallow's tail
Lands on the railing by surprise—
In a split second just the turn of it—
Mt. Fuji awakens and
Clean laundry is in the mountain air.

The day of unforgiving summer
Will grow even hotter—
Wet skin and the scent
Of cicada and shiny ginko leaves.

As it flies off—
Diagonal feathers in flight—it will
Go to its nest
In the heat of day
Of white breast and slender jet coat
And a gorging point
Of still red.

GINZA IN JUNE

The district's fabulous,
Wide boulevards open at the intersection,
A great electric mouth—
Skinny women
in provocative shoes with pointed heels
elegant windows and couples catch the eye—
a waning breeze and the sun
at their backs.

On the east corner the expensive shop—
Wagashi, maple syrup
Oranges and a clutter of black grapes,
Of the gift she sends
To the distant stranger.
      A slight romance of sky—
The sweet poison
Of this beautiful city.

KATSUNAMA: WINE COUNTRY

She straightens
In front of the heirloom, preparing for first tea

Tying her pale teal kimono—
With haste

Minutes later Kazu arrives
Smelling of rich clay

And overripened grapes—
A sublime face from a Turgenev novel

At a makeshift table
An organic circle forms

Methodically, she has arranged crisp miyogi
And white rice

Peach-colored sweets
And little dishes of stuff;

Pickled plums
And perfectly formed cakes of baked tofu

By nightfall they chat softly
In their native tongues;

The tallest beauty
Of the farming accident

And skating and the break on the ice
The winter before.

SLEEP

Hiragana is the night
Star time passes—
Thoughts of swallows.
      Each day a meaning—
The weight and intention
Of this hiding crescent
Above field of new sown rice;

I can see the moon from here
In the cooling night,
The cat says.

ANTICIPATION

Before the awaited call from home.
For nearly an hour high winds and lightning
Rattle window and flash silver across the night sky.
      Headlines from Kyushu: rescue, *six fatalities*
And a flood.
Telling like a jovial boy
The native says, *the mountain won't*
Protect us. You'll have to wear
Long, rubber boots—up to here, for the water.
Now closer the storm
This side of Fuji—
A call—
A minor quake.

NEW PLUMS

I want the tea hot
enough for the thick, green foam—
the iron kama still cold.

New tatami; the crane's neck vase

on the tokonoma
displays a hearty hydrangea this beginning June
after the rains.

Later
he puts out the brown paper bags
stuffed with plums—

    already a glassy flesh.
    We sort and choose as he talks
    to the palace's aid; a request:

blue plums
for the emperor.

    A wandering child in the village
Holds a catcher's net—
each day learning about catching new time
and the strangeness
of mountain butterflies.

    Today was hard before the medicine;
a smile at the farmer for the first time
and the widow's story: the Japanese Goddess
who sails a ship
to the shores of Korea on a boat

with a beautiful sail made of linen—
and the shy neighbor,
waiting for the potato buds to struggle
and break soil.
    The school children see robins today too—
a good sign
of the end of something delicate
and powerful.

HIROSHIMA BRIDGE

The nearest station
in town is home to dark, pragmatic birds,
pecking amongst the gravel
A few large ones perch the edge
of the temple-fashioned roof
I recall images of Italian copulas—
learning by contrast
       behind the structure awaits the
          Seto Inland Sea.
In the opposite direction: a moment of bridge
embraces the flatness
of translucent wave
and the sometimes invisible
glistening rock
that small sailboats
emerge from—
a trick of eye, and the theatre
of more intermittent sun
and a haunting
of a scene in a dream
back in time.

SADAKO'S RIDDLE

A universal story repeats
or anchors into the mind
of the Swedes, the Peruvians, the Nubians,
the students from Spain, the Americans from California—
all who wait to meet
the grey matrix stone of her.

At the bomb victim's memorial:
The unexpected sublime form
of a pubescent girl
looking off into a divine sky.
      Yet, hidden from the eye
the joy and persistence
Of her numbered cranes—defiance
the skill to fly
above any form
and action and blood.

MASAHIRO'S BEACH

White sand and shore meet horizon.
The salt company
In eye's view imposes
A memory of crystals,
nothing else.

> *I sit under the full bloom of white canopy*
> *and imagine him seeing me telepathically. I am someone else.*

As the water moves, faces
Emerge out of the flat
Collage of the scene. Near afternoon
We meander
And consider the tinge of cloud.

    Along for the trip; a foreigner and a mother—
A curious boy child.
The elder stands farthest away
Closest
To the strangest rock
Following his metaphysical play
As the umbrella snapshot softens
The crash
Of rising wave.

DINNER GUEST
for the hibakusha

I remember; he speaks, waiting his turn of sake
The wine of the gods, in an almost unintelligible tongue—
His tongue.

The translator is official
and obligatory in all black,
across the wide table
Overlooking the window view of the groomed white-sand garden
that swirls to meet
the seawall.

Speaking into the eyes
of the lovely, dark foreigner:
That day I was a schoolboy
when it all changed—
When the sun
came to earth.

NEARLY CHRISTMAS

We'll pound mochi on New Year's Day
As she places
The new sensei's ornament
On the near
Naked pine—
Silver, filigree at its center—
A crimson.
Her, in front
Of the slender slip of curtain—
A slow daylight
Fusing
With the small piano.

TEA LESSON AT DUSK

From the arrival
Of the child with his young mother

the smell of old wood
Is dark and reaches for the light

Just past the stone
Water basin with fresh water

That startles her skin.
The lotus in the untended garden

Has died. The instruction
Is almost silent—

The sound of hot water
While the master only gestures

With her hands
that are near

translucent from age.

A bloom
Three brisk petals of chrysanthemum—

a contiguous stem
Pointing east.

AUTUMN COMES

The bells are corrupt
and ring too
early in the blue, brush-covered mountains.

The old praying man loves
his brewed intoxications
lusting for the stranger—
a tenacious voyeur for most
of early summer.
        Before the sweets in celebration of the August ripe moon
a shadow in the pitch
of light—
a passing sleeve near
the garden maple.

WINTER: LEARNING TO BE TOUGH

Two middle-school boys
enjoy their wild masturbations
at lunchtime—
it keeps them warm
       In the dead of cold
heart and flesh joined solid.
Three plain girls
withstand the classroom freeze by creative anger;
they collect stickers—
alien girls who look like werewolves
and draw scarlet-headed ones
that look like neither of them
with eyes like beams
of sun.

REBEL

The world will end
on the island they were told—
proof of it; the Jizo
raised onto stone alters in the cobbled streets
leading to the City Hall building.
He didn't believe
it—
Always tormenting things, dreaming

To be a baseball star
He wanted to kill something.
He knew all
the secret places,
and made traps
The island boys nicknamed him:
the rice king.

THE KIMONO MAKER

The Empress was wearing the usual scarlet robe, under which she had kimonos of light plum, light green and yellow rose.

On that day all the ladies in attendance of his Majesty had taken particular great care with their dress. One of them, however, had made a small error in matching the colors at the opening of the sleeves.

—From the diaries of Shikibu Murasaki
Heian Era (1068–1167)

Before the time
Of the floating world
Ehime's twelve-layered juni-hitoe was all possibilities for the villagers
Of the iris month—
A gift and contest for the Shogun's affection
The kimono maker was masterful—
The dyer of silk
Dried months earlier
For hours sitting—
Eyes
At the loom
Connecting threads
To make the whole cloth.
      The garment for Ehime
Would follow the rule
Of garment:
Top garment
Over garment
Of twelve layers of silk.
    There were panels of cloth to consider;

The back of body
The back midseam
The hem, sleeve
Below armhole, back of sleeve—
Sleeve opening.
        And carefully there would
Be front of sleeve, the sleeve's width
The shoulder's width
Armhole seam.
Opening under armhole seam:
Collar, over collar
Length under collar and the front of body
Yet, it was
The spirit of the thing—
        This is Junko's ability. She considered the season—
The textures of things—
The magic of fire, wind, earth
And air.
But, it would be
The wearer—
A picture of painted waves
Of sea—
The first layer
Of outer garment
The symbol of the wearer—
Myriad colors
Of blue ink
Stitched into
A single garment.
The second layer
Would be seaweed-green

The third summer-squash yellow
The fourth eggplant indigo.
The fifth a shell pink
The sixth lemon yellow
The seventh winter grey
The eighth rose pink—
And ninth turquoise
And gold, lapis.
And the last layer would be the first
And then she would
Paint the moon
Of milk and dark amber.

DIALOGUES

(1)

Barcelona, I went in summer;
It's the prelude conversation to the elusive tale
About the museum.
        We're halfway of the ascent
That intersects with a meandering, clear stream—
Its beginning always returning to the origin
That bleeds into the granite.
        Famous for its modern look
Then its talk about Gaudi, Romare Bearden and the Japanese artist
On exhibit
        [Amassed along a full wall
        Of wooden shelves are configurations
        Of collectables during his residence there—
        Stuff from Germany and the stuffed
        Rabbit in lederhosen and a large, black-faced, cotton-
        stuffed doll with plentiful lips—
        Wild eyes and kinky hair
        Fashioned from yarn]

(2)

She speaks
A flower is a thing that has an intrinsic
Nature that determines its beauty
The first arrangement; the branches
are forced into direction to correspond
to its center.
An orchid has a different nature

than an iris wildflower—
While she watches the exercise, the memory
of the wounded dog
brought from the street—
its terrible suffering.
Just past noon
the flowers
have conformed into
wonderous shapes with
varied blooms.

(3)

Akiko struggles in shy, broken English—
I just understand the word kanshii for sad—
Like the sound of a blue note, I think.

A long time ago
Two unwed sisters once lived here,
this untouched beach
Of bleached sands;

A Tea man came to their remote hut
An errand
Sent by the Imperial Court.
They both fall
In love with him.
He leaves
Never to be seen again.

(4)

The little path to the observatory
Is weedy and seems to highlight

The austerity of it
>   *Closed.*

Disappointed, we meander back toward the nearest
Lit building on the resort. Inside we hear
Beautiful Japanese—slow and measured.

He talks
To the small audience half hidden in dark—
His pitch changing slightly as he recognizes
The black and brown couple.

I'm hungry—
our reason to escape into the milky, black night
About what?
The evolution of stars.

(5)

Elder students are chanting in unison.

After, Momoko begins:
From the center of your body; she moves the red silk tea napkin
Near the edge of her left knee
An isosceles.

They imitate her movement
beneath the hard light.
The hidden voice behind the soft sheath of screen;
the best noodles from Hokkaido
She boils the soba
and adds ginger.

(6)

At Onomichi the cherry blossom trees
Effuse a pink haze that paints itself onto a canvas
Of pristine white sky—
A spectacular melancholy.

We begin on the path of cherries beyond
The closing realm of sky; *he's now a great sumo wrestler*
She points to the stone engraved with his words:
> *Courage cannot measure the true champion*

Yuki is a kind of mystic, I think.

(7)

A discovery in an old antique shop
Near the sea front; a soft, wooden box
With Chinese ideograph: a bird whose roundness
Is poised on a spring branch emitting
A sweet
and strident sound.

And the accidental meeting of the raven
On the road;
> *Hello Mr. Raven*

Mechanically moving its head—
Seemingly severed
from its talent of sound.

(8)

You must see the exhibit
At the sushi café, a Nina Simone song plays ...
About that artist;

My favorite painting of her is her standing with a contented smile
arms crossed,
wearing something not so cute,
on top a world globe, with a backdrop of apricot canvas—
her rising from a torrent sea with a bloody knife,
peering at a woman in an Edo-style kimono
with her ring-pierced nipple exposed.

(9)

Her small chadogu shop survives
After the fire bombs from the war
        Tokyo looms *like a great urban monster*
The master seamstress tells her old friends after a day's work.
Remembering, she tells
Her student: *Know the true shape of the jar before you dress it—*
The spirit of the thing.

(10)

The cicadas blind the afternoon with sound—
unending
The arduous cycling uphill—
in the glare of sun.
The shop owner's
local peaches are ripe;
        What kind of fish is this? I ask
        Remembering the taste of my father's catfish
        from the Ohio River.
        He doesn't understand my English
        and instead points out a special sauce.

From an outdoor stage
the musicians carry their drums.
like Sisyphus heaving stone on sweating backs
By the time the tourists
have all gone from the shrine—
a break in the heat.

GEISHA'S DISCOVERY

She held the German songbook:
Der Zupfgeigenhansl; under the epigram, 1917
As though she had ventured
The sweeping countryside, tasted the fräulein's dumplings—
Saw a greenfinch in the Japanese countryside.
      And then the sudden sinking—
The knowing that heart pursues
Experience, will not deny
The reality: absence is not a trick
Of mind—love requires the body, belief,
The exact shared moment,
Of the performance of flowers.

SUNLIGHT FROM THE NORTH VIEW

The change of tea
        bowl
From ice blue
With a dusty hue—
The caddy holding firm
Under a half shadow;
        The radio host's voice
        animates the light,
        speaking melodious conversation
        about morality.

AT RECITAL

After 3:00,
The foreigner's voice
Was the color of smoke and late summer sun;
Her friend played *into* the keys
As she sang
For the children—
Eri San dressed in a green kimono
With loose obi.

Afterwards, she prepared American crackers with
A tart cheese
[Program Notes
Burleigh's tunes
Deep River
Sometimes I Feel Like A Motherless Child]

KYOTO

In the delicate and winding garden paths
Of the famous golden temple
Is a small pond
That remembers something about them.
The other African couple and her named Posey,
      Their eyes meeting—
His soft cotton attire, the loving disagreement near the stone replicas.
      The gods are sure of it:
Their impressions in the still flow
Of its scintillation
Bamboo and the summer camellia
A fire under water.

INTERSECTION

Roppongi subway, the foreigner's hub
in the city
is the long-ago cross point
of Basho—
the restless haiku poet
who died young.
Here, I envision the black Brazilian
standing on the exact spot
of the head of the precarious trail
where he walked
along sedges of tofu
toward the *Tsubo* Stone
on the sight of the Taga Castle.

Now, in my mind
the foreigners move
with purpose too—
the woman with the single, thick braid down her back
wearing the Indian shawl.

Maybe the Brazilian is the ephemeral poet
incarnated speaking Basho's words:

>*Sadly, I part from you;*
>*Like a clam torn from its shell,*
>*I go, and autumn too.*

PART III

San Francisco, 1993–2000

The words loved me, and I loved them back.
　　　　　　—Sonja Sanchez

MILLS COLLEGE: CONTEMPLATING POTTERY

Spring blazing
On the low residence windowsill,
Nothing grows from it.
Void of festival or rhyme—
Nothing to do with horses
Or the quickness of them.

No, not a Balinese one
With configurations
Of foaming vines
And tragic masks, but just naked
Stone made for wear,
And something accomplished.

GATHERING
for siblings

[early evening]
Tender. *She turns. Flowing*
Braids and the color of blue winterberries.
Two Kwanzas ago
She was the Virgin Mary
And talked about Unity. I asked:
Africa's head returned to its body?
Hips moving to the soul beat. *The beat.*
Deep down. *Arms stretching.*

Something misreferenced
Because of conversation, harmonious
Singing and her red velvet cake!
He is like a leaning tower
And struggle.
It's in the beat. The beat.
Faces laugh and love succeeds.
He is writing numbers
That look like the alphabet
Again.

MEI LEI (1967)

front photo page
the world changes;
a twelve-bodied sculpture;
children bent
from torso, overlapping a buttock
turned as meat, caked in white—
limestone,
in a gentle roadside ditch.

they lie open and comic
bloated from
hacking shells,
a child seems to pull loose
the limbs
of its mother, seed eyes to sky
      organs of jelly.

did they fall
in a heap
then turn
to sugared flesh?

EXCAVATING WATER; ARS POETICA

Let flow the word
Liberate the line
The facts—smithing in the light
And the dark
              Pushing for the right slant
A ruthless, beautiful making.
Weaving truth across
Fresh border,
Being the mountain
—groundwater.

The contemplative poet
The bridge of nations.

READING PROSE

You tried to guess
Scientifically
The tart surprise
>Strawberries?
>Kiwi?

No
Even after narration
The life
Of Nella Larsen
Who wrote
>*Quicksand*

And Sojourner
Who stood
As granite
And shouted,
>"Ain't I a Woman?"
>Peaches?

No
But later,
When we coupled
And something
Broke
Became electric
And darkly fluid
The tune stopped
And the silence answered,
"Blueberries."

TWIN ARTIFACT

The amber, slate striations
Solidify a broken pyramid against

The milky sill. She reflects: The rock is something solid,
Clear from the fog

That hangs over the Frenchman on the granite stallion.
The rock is more lucid—

Philosophy in *real time*
Remembering monks that covet the staffs embossed

On the almost lurid tapestry
With open and closed fuchsia petals and the lascivious

Demon attached
To the cloak of the benevolent. They are Africa meeting

Medieval voices while under the next portal
An aboriginal spirit soaks onto the face of the eucalyptus.

The fused
Dots mix with clay and light. The capillaries

Of landscape
Strike tune with feather strokes
From elbow. They listen and depart.

LIKE LANTERN

        girl body
scent of chalk
        and burning roses rhyming
and hexagonal.

there!
of boats
they tap
        and cowrie,
boy/dipping
kisses, paprika
obscuring

dipper afar
        on porch
ancestral

and milliner under florescent
bulb and elder bee

she/he/I negotiating lotus
near first beach.

A WEDDING SONG
For Myra & Abdul

The yam
Is the tender bride
Its taste ripe
And fills the hungry stomach.

The yam
Is the groom with strangled roots
Its shape anticipating
And heavy.

The yam
Is the family
Of the bride and groom—
The sliced body
For all to savor.

The yam
Is the burning sun—
A bridge,
A willow.

NEAR SEVEN

pepper
       cauliflower
jasmine
       astragalus root
tomatoes
  oats
   maple
lover's day suit
sage
lemon
       ginger
       couscous fine
barley
maize
      apples
a kiss divine!

1966

milk flows   children of the night
learn the secret of hearts   everything
wants to be opened.
she loses night
on the other track
stark patch
of ripe grass, an unturned sediment.
she massacres
everything she ever read
confuses
animals with breathing men
mixing blood
like squeezed grapes,
brown body
disconnects from stars.

NELLA'S EYES

You said something about Billie Holiday's voice
Burned. And I think of Nella
Before the photographer's lens.

Lace encircling her pale neck, a thin
ornament in the hollow of her throat,
    "Look this way, turn, lift your head"
Her eyes trapped for a splintered second—
The light shutter,
Released.
The fighting bird,
Electrocuted.

ON THE ISLAND
(Sapelo Island off the Coast of Georgia)

I.

His basket made from sweetgrass
weaves something from the island's
history;
their kin walked back to Sapelo
from the sea,
from beyond the Atlantic
and the middle door.
His name is Allan Green;
the surname conjures the natural green
of the place
Hog Hammock
that runs to meet the lips
of the water's edge,
splitting north and south.
Respect for the dead
is in their actions,
and blind memory
is replaced with real memories like Matty's
who tells
the visitor about
the dance hall
she loved
as a girl—the tub drums
and the mouth organ, rotting
with dust in a
hidden closet.

And Allan recalls
like an eager child
his boyhood mirage,
Blackbeard Island:
did they understand freedom
as returning—the flesh responding
to the first separation—
the soul always returning to Africa,
the body asunder.

II.

Bilali's first bargain
is now the life tree
of the island.
The scholar slave's
bloodline
can be traced
to all its members.
His knowledge of the long staple—
black-seed cotton—
soon became
his master's wealth
and his own—
one long prayer.
And the bond wisdom
of the tall African
and his blessed daughters:
Magret, Bentoo, Chaalut, Madina,
Yaruba, Fatima and Hestah.

Bentoo's grave now reads: "Minto Bell"

Her song goes:
she swell the rice to bloom—
drum it soft
give it life for the body—
the honey make us remember
our mother ties.

She swell the rice to bloom—
Drum it soft
Give it life for the body—
The honey make us forget
Our bitter eyes.

AUTUMN LANDSCAPE
A sestina

Deep bright are the veiled mountains.
The sheer lace of the speckling rain
floats the weight of gulls.
Further along the battered tracks,
silver intaglios in persimmon and taupe.

Human voices in the lungs of the railcar. Embers
and spaced forgetting are configured with the mountains.
Moving into view, reclining hills and suddenly taupe—
the balance of laughter frees repressed rain.
Nothing changes but perspective, speed and track
Harmonizing hills lain on their hips, satiny as gulls.

At noon a mother speaks to her child who watches gulls:
"This is the ocean here." And now we as ship of beet-colored embers,
water curls from crown of earth, obscures track.
Fast, without tenderness, tree masses block mountains,
erasing railcar, tearing smoke sky and rain,
inking out the railcar's name in stale yellow on its base marked "grand taupe."

The light on the small child turns from ash blue to gold.
With direction, mean-spirited white gulls
hover the railcar that pushes deeper into the rock and rain,
dipping into long graces with glowing embers.
"This point is connection to all ways north beyond the mountains,"
the conductor calls out dumbly, less alert of track.

All is less vibrant. Murky slate, unwinding track,
never ending, pulling forward, the child the single taupe.

Fence and salmon water tubs replace mountains—
steel mimics rocks, cuts natural shapes, murders gulls.
The lone figures and dull cement trace out disappearing embers
here, only the sound of cluttered patterns of clear rain.

FOLLOWING SPRING PATH

Running points burst ethereal yolks
at midday. Their satin-leaf boleros and purple cloaks—
from their bases obscene.
Unlike the tart sweet of tomato vines
Along rutted road, rehearsing old memory—
restraining from sun.

Up ahead two dark beauties. One bloom of each sex.
Hiding not to look
at the olive-branched matador
dissipating particle. The sun shifts.
The yolks lose their vibrancy—
bobbling rototillers
in hazy fields of beady heaven.

A brutal outcropping of canopy—
a back road
playing still, illuminating the children's gate.
Near highway the opposite end of sacred field
and the flagpole.
Further, progressively spent blossoms
soon drop. Self-effaced clover—
intrudes delicate faces
choked by running weed.

Finding the obscure garden.
The plain pots are liberated
from the lush lilies prostrate
on the green slime, dressing the laconic
fountain. The greenhouse path is too narrow

and disconnects from
the blushing trail of daffodils.
Almost. Late afternoon. Poignant
acorns scatter
ugly with tender wounds. Aggressive clusters
along the strip of eucalyptus,
a necessary poison
for the dwarfed birds.

KENTUCKY SUNFLOWER

For poet Jean Toomer (1894-1967)

O, stout sunflower
In my orange clay eyes
Like a child god,
quiet and bending
rustling with the tender rod.

Sing me the petal
That tingles
Like the sound of dawn
And hums the secret
Of the old psalm.

O comely sunflower
When the sun spills smoke
Over the eastern horizon—
And hot morning fog,
Sing me home
Ripe and sweet,
Like the cornstalk cob.

PRETTY WOMEN

Twin giraffe souls
striding on the summer boulevard;
a majestic sight—
soothing to the tired southern eye.

Jet shiny moving curves—
sinewy, tight
twist your bouncing
necks my way—
your daytime teasing night.

TO BE AFRAID

Is to wear your mother's
Sadness around your neck
And forget your name
Until god appears
With her hand out
And you cling
To her dress-tail
Till your heart
thaws.

DIVORCE ELEGY

Our
Best days
Crush forward
Like the smell
Of fresh basil
In spring.

CHANCE

Don't pass me now
When the wind
Is just right,
When the sail
Is at an angle
That moves us toward
A monument
Of plenty
And we covet
The thought of cruising
On a slow
Soprano wave.

Not now
When our palatial shore
Is crystalline
From a distance
And your copper knowledge
Is unearthed
And the watchtower
Hangs tangerine
On our voodoo horizon.

POET TO STUDENT

You are trans/ferring spirit
To paper
You are trans/ferring spirit
To paper
You are trans/ferring spirit
To paper,
Listen.

RITES OF PASSAGE

Brave, exiled priest
Standing is your legacy.
Bury deep
The love of your past
In this place of:
>*the singing*
>*the anguished praying*
>*the vigilant watching*
>*the hanging from branches*
>*in the black night,*
>*the secret teachings*
>*the preaching*
>*the building*

And to your brother:
Dreamer
Mystic
Of mistral eyes,
Sifting bone's history
From bare
Alter.

GLOSSARY

adzuki	a Japanese red bean
bon odori	a Japanese traditional dance to celebrate the dead
calligraphy	decorative handwriting or handwritten lettering
chadogu	a traditional tea utensil
chawan	a tea bowl
chozubashi	a stone water basin
cicada	a cricket
daikon	a Japanese radish
Edo	a period in Japanese history
geisha	an artist
ginko	a revered species of tree
Ginza	a famous shopping district in Tokyo
hibakusha	atomic bomb victims of Japan
hiragana	one of three Japanese syllabaries
Jizo	a Shinto folk shrine
juni-hitoe	a type of kimono
kabin	a vase
kaki	a persimmon
kama	an iron kettle
kanshii	sad
kibishi	strict, disciplined
kimonos	traditional women's dresses
kore	the reference meaning "there"
Kyoto	the traditional cultural center of Japan
Kyushu	a far south prefecture of Japan
matcha	Japanese powdered green tea, often used ceremoniously
miyogi	a Japanese onion-like vegetable
mochi	a traditional Japanese rice cake

nandina bamboo	a species of bamboo that grows red berries
noh	the oldest form of traditional Japanese theatre
obi	the sash worn with the kimono
oki ni	something that is repeated, in interval
Onomichi	a city in central Japan, famous for cherry blossoms
origami	traditional Japanese paper folding
Roppongi	a foreigner's district in Tokyo
sadako	a long-suffering victim of the atomic bomb blast
sakana	fish
sakana-ya	a fish shop
sake	a fermented rice alcoholic drink
sakura	the cherry blossom flower
samurai	a skilled Japanese swordsman
seihakuji	a traditional Japanese instrument
sensei	a teacher
seto	a traditional Japanese tea pottery
shoji	a traditional Japanese screen
sumo	a wrestler
taiko	a Japanese lead drum
tatami	traditional Japanese flooring made from a rice plant
tokonoma	traditional alter for displaying flowers and calligraphy
wagashi	traditional Japanese sweets

AUTHOR'S BIO

Yon Walls is also author of the Indie novel *Seeing Colette*, and the children's book anthology *African-American Children's Stories: A Treasury of Traditional Tales* adaptions *Two Ways to Count to Ten* and *The Magic Bones*. She's also author of the essay *The Cinematic Winter: Film and Working with Grief* in the book anthology *Seasons of Grief: Interventions for Bereaved People*. She holds a master's degree in Fine Arts in Creative Writing from Mills College and a PhD in Transpersonal Psychology. She's been writing poems since her teens and is interested in poetry as a human lived experience. She's taught poetry as an artist-in-residence to schoolchildren and adults as well as English and American Literature in Hiroshima, Japan. She currently lives in Santa Fe, New Mexico, and works with students from The Institute of American Indian Arts. She is also a long-term residence of Sacramento and the San Francisco Bay Area, California.

www.ingramcontent.com/pod-product-compliance
Lightning Source LLC
Chambersburg PA
CBHW010447010526
44118CB00021B/2534